Cloudy Days

by **Trudi Strain Trueit**

Reading Consultant: Nanci R. Vargus, Ed.D.

Marshall Cavendish
Benchmark
New York

Picture Words

 airplane

 barn

 bridge

 clouds

hot air balloon

 lighthouse

 mountain

 tree

Look! The sky is full of .

 float by an ✈.

 float by a .

 float by a .

10

 float by a 🎈.

12

 float by a ▮.

 float by a .

 float by a .

18

 float by me, too!

Words to Know

clouds (klowds)
    large groups of water droplets
    floating in the sky

float (floht)
    to move slowly through the air

Find Out More

Books

Herriges, Ann. *Clouds*. Minneapolis, MN: Bellwether
Media, 2007.

Rodgers, Alan. *Cloud Cover*. Chicago, IL: Heinemann
Library, 2007.

Webster, Christine. *Clouds*. New York, NY: Weigl
Publishers, 2007.

Videos

Reading the Clouds, Educational Video Network, 2004.

Tornado Intercept, National Geographic, Warner Home
Video, 2006.

Web Sites

**Iowa State University: Cool Clouds for Kids of All
Ages**
www.pals.iastate.edu/carlson/main.html

**University Corporation for Atmospheric Research
(UCAR): Web Weather for Kids: Clouds**
eo.ucar.edu/webweather/cloudhome.html

About the Author

Since childhood, Trudi Strain Trueit has been reading the sky. A former television weather forecaster for KAPP TV in Yakima, Washington, and KREM TV in Spokane, Washington, she wrote her first book for children on clouds. To date, she has written more than forty non-fiction titles for kids covering such topics as snow, hail, tornadoes, and storm chasing. Trudi writes fiction, too, and is the author of the popular *Julep O'Toole* series for middle grade readers. She lives near Seattle, Washington, with her husband and goes cloud watching whenever she can. You can read more about Trudi and her books at **www.truditrueit.com**.

About the Reading Consultant

Nanci R. Vargus, Ed.D., used to teach first grade. Now she works at the University of Indianapolis. Nanci helps young people become teachers. She enjoyed exploring all the plants and animals in the cloud forest in Costa Rica.

Marshall Cavendish Benchmark
99 White Plains Road
Tarrytown, NY 10591-5502
www.marshallcavendish.us

Library of Congress Cataloging-in-Publication Data
Trueit, Trudi Strain.
Cloudy days / by Trudi Strain Trueit.
     p. cm. — (Benchmark rebus. Weather watch)
Summary: "Easy to read text with rebuses explores clouds." Provided by publisher.
ISBN 978-0-7614-4011-6
1. Clouds — Juvenile literature. I. Title.
QC921.35.T784 2010
551.57'6 dc22
       2008046729

Editor: Christine Florie
Publisher: Michelle Bisson
Art Director: Anahid Hamparian
Series Designer: Virginia Pope

Photo research by Connie Gardner

Rebus images, with the exception of barn and bridge, provided courtesy of *Dorling Kindersley*.

Cover photo by Akira/amana images/Corbis

The photographs in this book are used by permission and through the courtesy of:
Getty Images: p. 2 Andrew Geiger (barn), Travel Ink (bridge); p. 19 Robert Postina; *The Image Works*: p. 5 Melaine Carr; p. 13 Classic Stock; *Art Life*: pp. 7, 21 age footstock; *Corbis*: p. 9 Richard T. Nowitz; p. 11 Roland Gerth; p. 15 Nik Wheeler; p. 17 Hans Strand.

Printed in Malaysia
1 3 5 6 4 2